Pebble Plus

Animal Offspring

Cows and Their Calves

by Margaret Hall

Consulting Editor: Gail Saunders-Smith, Ph.D.

Consultant: Steven Stewart, DVM
College of Veterinary Medicine, University of Minnesota
St. Paul, Minnesota

Capstone press

Mankato, Minnesota

Pebble Plus is published by Capstone Press
151 Good Counsel Drive, P.O. Box 669, Mankato, Minnesota 56002
http://www.capstone-press.com

1 2 3 4 5 6 08 07 06 05 04 03

Library of Congress Cataloging-in-Publication Data
Hall, Margaret, 1947–
Cows and their calves/by Margaret Hall.
v. cm.—(Pebble plus: Animal offspring)
Includes bibliographical references (p. 23) and index.
Contents: Cows—A calf—Growing up—Watch cows grow.
ISBN 0-7368-2105-8 (hardcover)
1. Calves—Juvenile literature. 2. Cows—Juvenile literature. [1. Cows. 2. Animals—Infancy.] I. Title. II. Series.
SF205 .H26 2004
636.2'07—dc21   2002155598

Editorial Credits
Sarah L. Schuette, editor; Kia Adams, series designer; Jennifer Schonborn, cover production designer;
    Kelly Garvin, photo researcher; Eric Kudalis, product planning editor

Photo Credits
Bruce Coleman Inc./Hans Reinhard, 13; Lynn Stone, 21 (right)
Index Stock Imagery/Lynn Stone, cover
Minden Pictures/Yva Momatiuk/John Eastcott, 1, 21 (left); Mitsuaki Iwago, 4–5; Jim Brandenburg, 18–19
PhotoDisc Inc., 20 (both)
Tom Stack & Associates/Bob Pool, 17; Joe McDonald, 10–11
Visuals Unlimited/Inga Spence, 7, 9; Patrick J. Endres, 14–15

Note to Parents and Teachers

The Animal Offspring series supports national science standards related to life science. This book describes and illustrates cows and their calves. The images support early readers in understanding the text. The repetition of words and phrases helps early readers learn new words. This book also introduces early readers to subject-specific vocabulary words, which are defined in the Glossary section. Early readers may need assistance to read some words and to use the Table of Contents, Glossary, Read More, Internet Sites, and Index/Word List sections of the book.

Word Count: 109
Early-Intervention Level: 12

Table of Contents

Cows

Cows are mammals. Cows have black, brown, white, or red hair. Young cows are called calves.

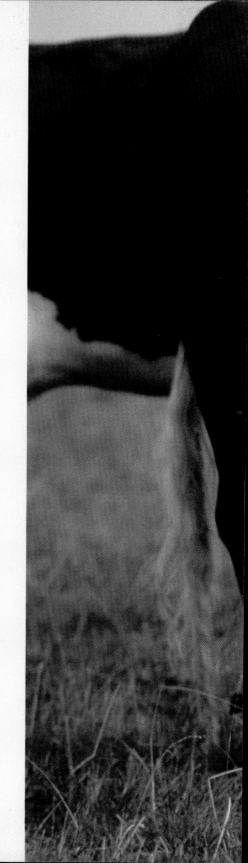

Cows and calves graze
in pastures on farms and
ranches. Cows and calves
sometimes live in barns.

A male is a bull. A female is a cow. Bulls and cows mate. A calf begins to grow inside the cow.

The Calf

The cow gives birth to a calf. The cow takes care of the calf.

Calves have long legs. Calves can stand up about one hour after they are born.

Calves drink milk from
their mothers.

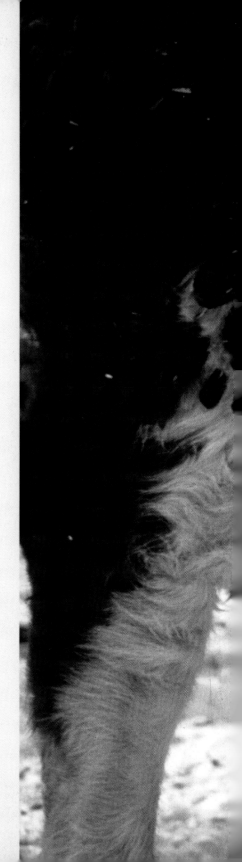

Growing Up

Calves start to eat hay,
grass, and grain after
about one month.

Calves become adults after about two years.

Watch Cows Grow

birth

adult after about two years

Glossary

birth—the event of being born; cows usually give birth to one calf at a time; cows sometimes have twins.

bull—an adult male of the cattle family; bulls can father young; male calves that do not become fathers are called steers.

cow—an adult female of the cattle family; a young cow is called a heifer before she gives birth to a calf for the first time.

graze—to eat grass and other plants that are growing in a pasture or field

mammal—a warm-blooded animal that has a backbone and hair or fur; female mammals feed milk to their young.

mate—to join together to produce young; cows give birth nine months after mating.

pasture—land that animals use to graze

Read More

Murphy, Andy. *Out and About at the Dairy Farm.* Minneapolis: Picture Window Books, 2003.

Powell, Jillian. *From Calf to Cow.* How Do They Grow? Austin, Texas: Raintree Steck-Vaughn, 2001.

Taus-Bolstad, Stacy. *From Grass to Milk.* Start to Finish. Minneapolis: Lerner, 2003.

Trumbauer, Lisa. *The Life Cycle of a Cow.* Life Cycles. Mankato, Minn.: Pebble Books, 2003.

Internet Sites

Do you want to find out more about cows and their calves? Let FactHound, our fact-finding hound dog, do the research for you.

Here's how:

1) Visit *http://www.facthound.com*

2) Type in the **Book ID** number: **0736821058**

3) Click on **FETCH IT.**

FactHound will fetch Internet sites picked by our editors just for you!

Index/Word List